Town Animals

**Written and Illustrated
by Vera Croxford**

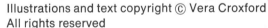

Illustrations and text copyright © Vera Croxford
Library of Congress catalog card number: 77-71
ISBN: 0-448-14283-X (Paperback Edition)
ISBN: 0-448-13009-2 (Library Edition)
First published in the United States by
Grosset & Dunlap, Inc., New York, N.Y. 1977
Published by arrangement with
Transworld Publishers Ltd., London
Printed and bound in the United States of America

Grosset & Dunlap   **A Filmways Company**   **Publishers**   **New York**

Many animals live in the country, others find

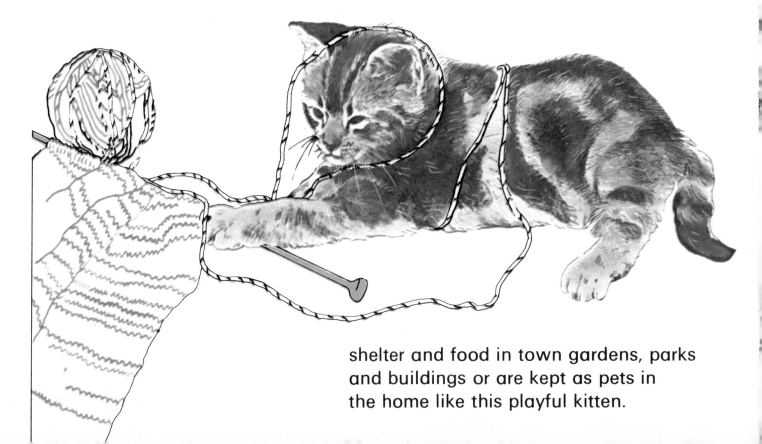

shelter and food in town gardens, parks
and buildings or are kept as pets in
the home like this playful kitten.

Home

Mother dog feeds and cares for her puppies until each one is old enough to leave her and go to a new home. The cat can smell house mouse down her hole.

House mouse collects Father's wood shavings, Mother's knitting wool and other scraps and makes her nest with them under the floor.

Garden

A bird table is visited by many birds if wholemeal bread, cheese, fat and peanuts are put out. Fresh coconut is only goo[d] in the winter as it is harmful to baby birds. Bir[ds] also need water to drink [and] bathe in.

Blackbird

Robin

Blue Tit

Song thrush

If berried shrubs and trees grow in the garden Song thrush will enjoy eating the berries and may also eat the snails that feed on the vegetables.

A nest box fixed in a high place, safe from cats, hot sun and rain may encourage robins to nest, or they may nest in the garden shed.

Nest box

Robin cleans her nest in the shed.

Great Tit on a coconut.

Garden

Rabbit sleeps in the clean hay inside his large hutch. He likes to be gently stroked and lifted with both hands, one placed under his rump. He finds it very painful to be lifted by his ears.

The flowers use their colour and scent to attract insects. Honey bee sips nectar and collects pollen for the hive. Peacock butterfly sips nectar with her long tongue and seven spot ladybird hunts aphids.

Honey bee

Seven spot
ladybird

Peacock
butterfly

Horse

The rag and bone man collects old clothes and furniture from homes with his horse and cart. Blue Tit pecks off tree bark when hunting for insects and pecks off milk bottle tops to sip the cream. Red fox searches a town dustbin for food.

The policeman's horse helps him
to control large crowds of people.
Pigeons nest on ledges of buildings
and feed on scraps of food found in
the streets or are fed by people.

Police horse

Pigeons

The blind woman's dog has been trained to guide her safely through crowded streets and across busy roads when she goes shopping.

Guide dog

Market

Black rats live in markets and warehouses. They often chew open sacks to eat the vegetables and grain which then cannot be sold. Kittiwakes usually nest on cliffs but can be seen on ledges of a warehouse.

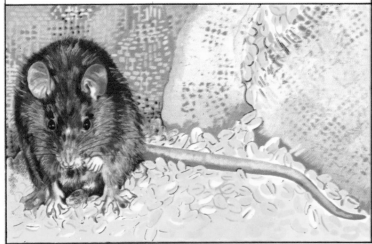

Black rat
eating grain.

Nesting
Kittiwakes

Buildings

White storks are welcomed each spring by the villagers of Rust who believe the birds will bring them luck. They help the storks build nests and feed their young.

Family of white storks.

Kestrel hunts mice and sparrows. House martin made her mud nest under the eaves. Starlings roost in towns to keep warm and safe. The noise they make before sleeping is as loud as the traffic.

Kestrel   House martin   Starlings

Rubbish tip

Herring gulls look for food scraps in the rubbish. Sometimes stray dogs, no longer fed by their owners, search for food scraps.

Mute swan cleans and oils his feathers to keep them water-proof. Mallard duck is closely followed by her ducklings who are able to swim in the water soon after hatching.

Church yard

Barn owl

Barn owl young

Barn owl hunts a mouse at night and will feed it to her hungry young in the church tower. Banded snail moves slowly across a tomb stone. Common bat hangs inside the tower. Soon he will leave to hunt insects in the churchyard.

Banded snail

Common bat

Park

Many kinds of dog live in towns where there are few gardens to run in. The dogs' owners take them for long walks in the park to keep them healthy.

Hedgehog licks an ice-cream
carton dropped by a child
during the day. Grey squirrel
has found a nut. He lives in
an oak tree in the park.

Zoo

Giant panda

In a zoo you can learn about many kinds of animals. Tigers are rare because some men have hunted them for sport, killed their prey or taken their territory. Panda comes from the bamboo forests in China.

Young okapi was born in the zoo. Okapis are bred in captivity because they are rare in the African rain forests. Red and blue macaw from South America has learnt to say "hallo".

Okapi with young.

Red and blue macaw.

Moths on a sooty town tree.

Moths on a lichen covered country tree.

Tree

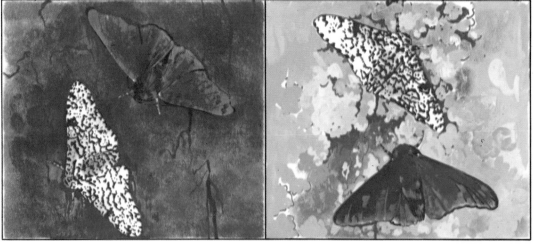

Peppered moths can be black or white. When black moths are found on a sooty town tree they cannot easily be seen and eaten by birds. They are camouflaged. Their colour is the same as the tree. White moths can easily be seen on a black tree but when they settle on a lichen covered country tree then they cannot be seen as easily as the black moth.

7.